WITHDRAWN

Careers in the US Air Force

Melissa Phillips

© 2016 ReferencePoint Press, Inc.
Printed in the United States

For more information, contact:
ReferencePoint Press, Inc.
PO Box 27779
San Diego, CA 92198
www.ReferencePointPress.com

Picture Credits:
Cover: US Air Force/Tech. Sgt. Jared Marquis
  6: Accurate Art, Inc
30: US Air Force/Mater Sgt. Ben Bloker
39: US Air Force/Staff Sgt. James L. Harper Jr.
45: US Air Force/Maj. A.C. Losurdo
59: US Air Force/Senior Airman James Richardson

LIBRARY OF CONGRESS CATALOGING-IN-PUBLICATION DATA

Names: Phillips, Melissa A., 1972-
Title: Careers in the US Air Force / by Melissa Phillips.
Description: San Diego, CA : ReferencePoint Press, Inc., [2015] | Series: Military careers | Includes
    bibliographical references and index.
Identifiers: LCCN 2015036314| ISBN 9781601529329 (hardback) | ISBN 1601529325 (hardback)
Subjects: LCSH: United States. Air Force--Vocational guidance.
Classification: LCC UG633 .P49 2015 | DDC 358.40023/73--dc23
LC record available at http://lccn.loc.gov/2015036314

Contents

"To Fly, Fight and Win"

The Air Force is the youngest branch of the military. It has only been around since 1947. As of June 2015 the Air Force had about 308,000 total active-duty personnel. A career in the Air Force may be the right choice for anyone interested in maintaining or flying aircraft and defending the nation in the air, in space, and even in cyberspace. According to the Air Force website, its goal is "to fly, fight and win." To accomplish this mission, this branch of the military is in charge of all types of aircraft that are responsible for protecting the nation. However, of the more than 300,000 total active-duty personnel, only 12,920 are pilots. This means only about 14 percent of the total Air Force population flies planes. All other members of this branch of service occupy aircraft or personnel support positions or take on other roles that help promote the mission of the Air Force.

Enlisted and Officers

The Air Force has more than 130 diverse careers for enlisted personnel. Both men and women serve in the Air Force. About 19 percent of Air Force personnel are women. The Air Force was expected to open all positions to women in 2016. Qualifying for a position in this military branch requires candidates to have either a high school diploma or a general equivalency diploma. Applicants also have to take the Armed Services Vocational Aptitude Battery (ASVAB). The Air Force breaks down the ASVAB into qualification areas: general, mechanical, administrative, and electrical. Using the scores to help find the best career field match, an Air Force job counselor provides a short list of job options. Sometimes there is a short wait before a job becomes available.

The Air Force has a standard enlistment promotion system based on the time an individual spends in both the service and in his or her specific pay grade. As the promotions in rank get higher, there are fewer positions available. Almost everyone graduates from basic training with an airman basic (E-1) rank. With more experience, training, and responsibilities, recruits can be promoted through the ranks to senior airman (E-4). From there, those who demonstrate the highest level of leadership and dedication to Air Force traditions and standards can earn the next rank promotion as an officer, becoming a staff sergeant.

All enlistees are required to fulfill a minimum two-year commitment on active duty and at least two years as an inactive ready reservist, which means being on call for duty in case of emergencies. After signing an enlistment contract, military life begins. This will require moving to Lackland Air Force Base for basic training, moving again for specialized career-field training, and at least one additional time to the base where an active-duty Air Force career begins.

Those who begin their Air Force career as officers are called *commissioned officers*. Officers must have at least a bachelor's degree and approval from a member of Congress. Some of the more advanced career fields in the Air Force, such as dentistry and psychology, require more advanced college degrees. Many commissioned officers begin their military career path by earning a degree from the US Air Force Academy or one of the Air Force Reserve Officers' Training Corps programs. More than 750 colleges and universities participate in these two-year programs. Another option is to attend Officer Training School after earning a traditional bachelor's degree. This five-week training program teaches all aspects of Air Force life to those who have not been exposed to military procedure through their college studies.

The Air Force also has what it calls a *stressed list* of enlisted and officer jobs that are in high demand but face shortages of qualified applicants. These positions include pararescue personnel, remotely piloted aircraft pilots, and air liaison officers. The stress level is based on several factors, including the number of vacancies that need to be filled and the number of seats for those specific jobs that are available in training centers. Recruits can often see more rapid promotion if they enter a stressed career path simply because the Air Force needs qualified individuals to take on those responsibilities.

US Armed Forces: Pay

In the US Armed Forces, pay for both enlisted personnel and officers depends on rank and years of service. Promotions depend on performance in addition to number of years served, with higher ranks translating to higher pay grades. The two graphs show monthly salaries commonly reached in the first four years of service.

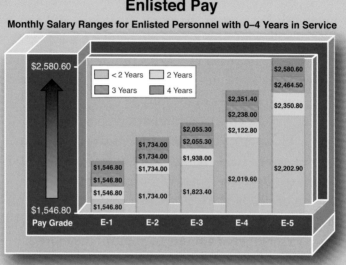

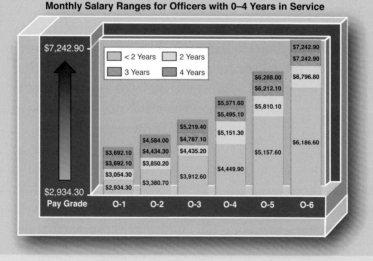

Note: Monthly salary ranges in both graphs are based on enlisted and officer pay scales effective January 1, 2015. The pay scales described here do not take into account the value of health benefits or housing and other allowances.

Source: Defense Finance and Accounting Service, "Military Pay Charts, 1949 to 2015," December 23, 2014. www.dfas.mil/militarymembers/payentitlements/military-pay-charts.html.

Many Possible Careers

The Air Force offers many career opportunities in generalized fields of interest that include arts and education, computer science, technology, and maintenance and repair. Within each of these fields are many areas of specialization. For example, a recruit interested in a career in logistics and transportation could coordinate takeoffs and landings as an air traffic controller, help pilots understand the stresses of flight as an aerospace physiologist, or fix engines as an aerospace propulsion expert. Technical Sergeant Frank McMahon III is an Air Force recruiter, the person responsible for finding young men and women who would be interested in joining up. In an article in *Airman* magazine, McMahon explains, "I love the Air Force, and I want other people to be able to experience what it has to offer." Of course, McMahon has to include his own position in the list of careers the Air Force has available. He notes, "We need to have recruiters out there, pounding the pavement and telling the Air Force story to young people. How else are they going to know about all the tremendous opportunities the service offers?"

As in all branches of the military, Air Force jobs have a range of entry-level requirements and opportunities for promotion to an officer's rank. The ASVAB score is also used as a tool to guide recruits into a field that best suits their abilities and interests. For example, a career as a logistics planner might be a good choice for someone who earns high scores in the sections of the test that assess coding skill, numerical operations, and verbal expression. Everything that happens in the Air Force requires planning and coordination. Logistics planners work behind the scenes to make sure missions run smoothly and service members stay safe. A high score in the mechanical sections shows potential for a job in helicopter, missile, and jet maintenance. Someone who scores high in verbal expression and arithmetic reasoning might do well as a cybersystems operations specialist. This job keeps the cyberspace network of communications secure from terrorists while making sure that all data is transmitted quickly and accurately. Finding the right career path in the Air Force is essential for success and satisfaction. Using tests like the ASVAB and listening to the advice of recruiters might help those interested make better decisions concerning which path to take.

Recruiters like McMahon recognize that there are fewer recruiters in the Air Force than there are in other branches of the service, so they must work harder to attract young people looking to serve their country. Despite the shortage of recruiters, McMahon says, "We keep making our goals. And we're recruiting the best and brightest." With such optimism, the Air Force anticipates it will continue to draw in recruits who are looking for a way to further their education, build a rewarding career, and satisfy a desire for adventure.

Psychologist

Air Force psychologists serve as valuable resources throughout an airman's or airwoman's career and often even after a person leaves the military. They have many duties and responsibilities, such as conducting intake assessments, diagnosing and treating mental disorders, facilitating individual and group counseling sessions, and evaluating pilots' mental health readiness for special missions. During the first week of basic training, psychologists evaluate new recruits to determine their ability to manage the physical and mental pressures of a military career. For those recruits who are suspected of being at high risk for mental health issues, a more in-depth evaluation is administered. A similar mental health evaluation is administered to determine a candidate's eligibility for special missions.

One of the major responsibilities of a psychologist is to evaluate, diagnose, and counsel or treat airmen and their families before, during, and after deployment. To prepare Air Force personnel for deployment,

At a Glance:
Psychologist

Minimum Educational Requirements
Doctorate in clinical or counseling psychology

Personal Qualities
Patient, compassionate, able to solve problems, empathetic

Certification and Licensing
Current license in clinical or counseling psychology

Working Conditions
In hospitals, clinics, community outreach centers, combat zones

Salary Range
Monthly salary depends on pay grade and years of service

Number of Jobs
As of 2009, 235 psychologists served in the Air Force

Future Outlook
12 percent job growth through 2022

9

psychologists teach preventive strategies to combat the anxiety, stress, and depression that can happen while on a tour of duty. They also provide techniques for avoiding self-destructive behaviors that may occur during and after wartime experiences. In the *Monitor on Psychology* article "The Career Path Less Traveled," Karen A. Orts explains her many roles and responsibilities as an Air Force psychologist. In addition to her counseling role, she also teaches senior noncommissioned officers at the Air University "how to prevent suicide, handle alcohol-related incidents and identify other potential problems among the men and women they lead."

Psychologists also support military families. Families sometimes experience anxiety and fear during extended deployments. Psychologists can provide counseling to help families adjust to these changes and teach healthy emotional coping skills during challenging times. Air force psychologists also help service members and their families adjust to life once deployments end. Post-traumatic stress disorder (PTSD) and chronic pain from serious injuries can make the transition from combat zone to home difficult, causing marital, relationship, and family problems. Individual or family counseling sessions, group therapy, or other assistance are all services provided by Air Force psychologists.

How Do You Become a Psychologist?

Education

High school students who have an interest in this career can prepare by taking psychology classes. They can also benefit from writing and speech courses because strong communication skills are essential for psychologists. Classes in high school biology might also be helpful, particularly in understanding the human brain.

Although these courses do not have a specific focus on military issues, the Air Force Junior Reserve Officers' Training Corps (AF-JROTC) program provides military experiences in high school. For students who are in grades nine through twelve and are interested in serving their country in the Air Force, many schools offer approved Air Force coursework through the AFJROTC. The curriculum focuses on leadership skills, policy and organization, character education, and aerospace sciences. This program prepares high school graduates to join the Air Force ROTC program at colleges and universities. College scholarships are available for tuition, textbooks, and a monthly stipend. Some of these scholarships require the recipient to serve up to four years active duty after graduation.

The job of psychologist requires a significant commitment to college-level coursework. After successfully completing an undergraduate program in psychology from an accredited university, the next step is to earn a master's degree and a doctorate in counseling or clinical psychology. Counseling focuses more on individual and group guidance and counseling while clinical psychology traditionally concentrates on mental health and illness. The majority of doctoral-level clinical and counseling psychology programs do not differ much, however; they offer the same licensure, the same internships, and very similar coursework.

Because a college education can be very costly, the Air Force offers full tuition through its Health Professions Scholarship program. All school fees, supplies, books, equipment, and living expenses are awarded to those individuals who have earned a bachelor's degree in psychology or a related field and have been accepted into or are currently enrolled in an accredited graduate or doctoral program in psychology as a full-time student. While in school, Air Force scholarship beneficiaries must serve forty-five days active duty each year and three years active duty after graduation. In the event that the scholarship recipient does not complete the program, active-duty service is required for each year that Air Force grant money was provided. The same three-year commitment is required for those who enter the Air Force after completing a doctorate in psychology without a military scholarship. Within either area of study, clinical or counseling, the doctoral program must include a one-year internship to meet Air Force entrance requirements. Although internship experiences can be in many different areas of practice, interested applicants should consider finding one that relates to military issues, such as PTSD.

After completing the required schooling, internship, and licensure, psychologists enter the Air Force as commissioned officers, where they begin their military career by completing a five-week Commissioned Officer Training program. Classroom instruction covers military life and the military health care system, leadership and teamwork skills, and Air Force policies and regulations. Even though most Air Force psychologists work in a traditional office environment or hospital setting, daily physical fitness training is a required part of the five-week program.

Certification and Licensing

An Air Force psychologist must have a doctorate degree in clinical or counseling psychology from an American Psychological Association accredited university and have completed a one-year psychology internship. An additional year of postdoctoral training is also required.

Volunteer Work and Internships

The first step on this career path is to begin by volunteering in high school programs. Best Buddies is an international volunteer movement in high schools across the world that provides leadership opportunities for high school students to develop friendships and mentor peers with intellectual disabilities. Peer mentoring and volunteering for a homework hotline are also opportunities for making a positive impact on others who need help.

Many colleges and universities offer programs to high school students who are interested in a career in psychology. For example, Gettysburg College in Pennsylvania hosts Camp Psych, which introduces the attendees to field of psychology, engages students in cutting-edge research, and provides real-world experiences. Another school, Columbia University in New York, offers summer courses, labs, and workshops to high school juniors and seniors on the fundamental theories of psychology, the foundations of human behavior, and current psychology issues relating to real-world events. One additional workshop geared to high school students in preparation for a career in the mental health field is offered by the Psychology Department at the Illinois Institute of Technology. In this workshop, students learn about human behavior across the life span and take part in group discussions and field trips.

Skills and Personality

Psychological services are often provided during stressful times, such as preparing individuals and families for deployment, counseling individuals with PTSD after they return from a tour of duty, and providing treatment for drug and alcohol abuse. Having empathy to understand and share someone else's feelings during emotional times, in order to provide therapy and support, is key to a job in the mental health field. As part of the Air Force, psychologists also must have strong analytical skills that assist in making difficult decisions such as determining whether someone is ready to return to active duty or is qualified to pilot a special mission. Through active listening, a good psychologist is able to piece together fragments of shared information to help patients work through their issues and problems. Airmen throughout the ranks share sensitive and confidential information that they trust will not be shared with anyone else in the Air Force. Upholding the American Psychological Association's Code of Ethics regarding confidentiality between patient and psychologist is a legal requirement for anyone in mental health practice and is also essential for building trusting relationships in a therapeutic setting.

In the 2015 online article "Mental Misconceptions: Psychologist's Mental Health Perspective," Captain Nancy DeLaney explains that she left her civilian position for a career with the Air Force because "here, people are encouraged to call a timeout. We can prescribe an hour of breathing exercises. We can have counseling sessions in the middle of the week. As professionals, we can help those people immediately, not just when it is the most convenient for the work schedule." Her interest is in preventive care, something the Air Force makes a top priority. DeLaney adds that she feels honored to help other people through their life's journey during difficult times.

On the Job

Working Conditions

Depending on where their services are needed and on their individual areas of expertise, the working environment of psychologists in the Air Force will vary. Many psychologists work in military hospitals or clinics located across the United States, although some are sent to medical facilities near US bases in other countries. Some psychologists travel overseas into war zones as part of combat stress control teams to provide counseling services to troops in the field.

Earnings

As with most jobs in the military, psychologist pay varies depending on years of experience and rank. However, the Air Force offers signing bonuses for many medical professionals, including psychologists. Free health care and military housing are also provided.

Opportunities for Advancement

Psychologists enter the military as a second lieutenant (O-1). After completing the five-week officer training program, promotion to first lieutenant (O-2) is almost always automatic. A board review process that includes a review of performance evaluations, assignment history, distinction and honors, and continuing education certificates is required for promotions to captain (O-3) and then major (O-4). As the officer ranking gets more advanced, the review process for promotion becomes more rigorous and competitive.

What Is the Future Outlook for a Psychologist?

With current regulations requiring military health insurance to include preventive and treatment-based mental health services, the Air Force has a high demand for qualified psychologists. Because of the rigorous requirements for this career, there are more jobs in the mental health field than there are qualified applicants. According to the USA-Jobs online job board for June 2015, there were multiple vacant positions for psychologists at 117 Air Force bases across the United States.

What Are Employment Prospects in the Civilian World?

With the projected job growth of approximately 12 percent through 2022 for those who have earned a doctorate in clinical or counseling psychology, job opportunities after leaving the Air Force are abundant. The practice of diagnosing and treating individuals and families affected by military-related mental health conditions such as PTSD, depression, and anxiety translates well into the private sector in a clinical or counseling practice. For psychologists like Orts who teach at the Air University, a natural progression may be transitioning into the civilian field of educational psychology with public and private colleges. Another option for employment in the civilian world is through the Department of Veterans Affairs. For example, a counselor uses experience and training learned during active duty to work with individuals and families to address ongoing problems associated with combat and related military experiences.

Operations Command website, Brown explains, "From intelligence, surveillance, and reconnaissance [aircraft] to fighters to bombers, some foreign as well; the whole gamut was participating in this event."

How Do You Become a Special Tactics Officer?

Physical Requirements

Before basic training, all candidates must pass the Physical Ability and Stamina Test, which includes swimming, running, sit-ups, and push-ups. After basic training, airmen must successfully complete the officer training program. In addition, they must have at least 20/40 visual acuity and not suffer from colorblindness, be between 4 feet 10 inches (147 cm) and 6 feet 8 inches (203 cm) tall, and weigh no more than 250 pounds (113 kg).

Education

Joining the Air Force Junior Reserve Officers' Training Corps (AF-JROTC) is the first step toward exploring an STO career. At Laurel Highlands High School in Pennsylvania, for example, one cadet each year is recognized with an Air Commando Association Award to increase awareness of the Air Force's special operations opportunities. At another high school's AFJROTC program in New Mexico, cadets participate in realistic physical training exercises at the local military base where special operations air commandos provide real-life experiences of what the Air Force has to offer. In the November 2014 Cannon Air Force Base newsletter, Technical Sergeant Thomas Canada explained that the purpose of these partnerships is to teach students "core values and leadership traits that will help [them] acclimate quicker to the demands of a military lifestyle."

This program prepares high school graduates to join the Air Force ROTC program at colleges and universities. College scholarships are available for tuition, textbooks, and a monthly stipend. Some of these scholarships require the recipient to serve up to four years active duty after graduation.

Candidates who wish to pursue a path toward STO must first

serve as an officer in the Air Force and then obtain a release from their current duties to complete the STO training program. In this intense and exhausting program, the chosen individuals will learn parachuting, diving, and combat training. This certification process takes two years to complete and comprises both initial and advanced training. The initial training program is composed of learning air traffic control communication procedures and traffic rules, wilderness survival skills, and combat zone parachuting skills. The next phase of instruction includes advanced parachute skills and aerial maneuvers, combat scuba diving, and simulated combat practice.

Skills and Personality

The job of STO is not an easy one. It is not for everyone. It takes leadership, professionalism, and dedication. STOs must be confident, mentally tough, and self-disciplined. Every day involves strenuous activity, with STOs mentally and physically training for or conducting missions. Technical Sergeant Jay Chambers, a special tactics instructor, was interviewed by *USA Today* magazine about what it takes to be part of Air Force special operations. "We're looking for the type-A personality, unusually aggressive, focused. We need somebody who's always wanted to succeed. People who don't want to do ordinary things. We're looking for the physically fit—the high school wrestler, track runners, swimmers." Solving problems in stressful situations is another vital skill. This job requires intelligence and creativity to overcome obstacles while always keeping the mission in sight. As one special tactics squadron commander states in an interview for the Eielson Air Force Base online newsletter, the characteristics required for leading a special tactics squadron include "absolute self-confidence, to the point where they are not afraid to make mistakes. A 'never quit' attitude."

Volunteer Opportunities

Dedication and leadership are key qualities the Air Force looks for in STO candidates. There are plenty of opportunities for students to develop these qualities while still in school. Creating or leading charity events or becoming a student ambassador for the Wounded Warrior Project—a nonprofit that benefits veterans and their families—are just a couple of the many ways students can show leadership and commitment. The skills necessary to create and run a charity event are the same skills needed for a special operations career. The Air Force also looks for so-called servant leaders to fill these positions. Servant leaders put the needs of others before their own. Volunteering at a food bank, blood drive, or other event that gives back to the community is a great way to develop this type of leadership skill.

On the Job

Working Conditions

STOs rarely have a traditional workday. They may be required to parachute into an active combat zone or scuba dive into hostile territory to look for buried explosives. These highly trained officers have to be ready for combat any time, day or night, anywhere in the world. The rigorous physical and mental training of STOs is designed to prepare them for most extreme situations. While stationed in Afghanistan, Major F. Damon Friedman and his team were tasked with conducting operations to keep the enemy from consolidating and launching an attack. "When we came in, there were about 100 enemy forces in the area. I was up for three days without a second of sleep conducting close air support with numerous aircraft overhead," Friedman recalled in an article on the Air Force Special Operations Command website. During this battle he saved the lives of his teammates by directing the delivery of 4,000 pounds (1,814 kg) of bombs and rockets using aircraft-mounted automatic weaponry only a football field's length away from his own troops. Such officers have to be cool under pressure and deal with high levels of stress as part of their normal duties.

Earnings

Although monthly salary depends on pay grade and years of service, STOs also qualify for hazard pay, parachute pay, and special duty incentive pay.

Opportunities for Advancement

Air Force personnel receive promotions based on a standardized process called the Weighted Airman Promotion System. When candidates become eligible for a promotion, they earn points based on pay grade, years of service, awards, decorations, performance reports, and scores on the Promotion Fitness Examination. Those who have the highest overall number of points earned are promoted; however, promotions also depend on open positions. STOs can advance through various officer grades as they earn the right and as those positions become available.

What Is the Future Outlook for a Special Tactics Officer?

A little over $9 million has been budgeted to fill vacancies in this high-demand position. Likewise, another $7 million has been allotted for bonuses to entice STOs to stay in the Air Force. All of this suggests a good future outlook for STOs.

What Are Employment Prospects in the Civilian World?

Like many other military careers that translate well into civilian employment, the skills used as an STO are similar to those required in law enforcement. For example, members of police tactical and SWAT teams take part in potentially volatile situations such as hostage negotiations and security, riot prevention and control, and high-risk arrests and assaults. STOs know how to manage such potentially dangerous situations calmly and effectively. In addition, private organizations actively recruit retired military special forces to lead training in law enforcement, weapons intelligence, and explosive ordnance disposal programs.

Mark Lauren, a retired STO, turned his skills into a profitable business by creating training programs and diets to fit the needs of clients. As a soldier, Lauren effectively trained more than seven hundred recruits for special operations. Using that expertise and experience to kick-start a civilian career, he became a fitness expert. In this role, he creates individualized diets and exercise programs, publishes fitness and nutrition videos and books, and has even designed a smartphone app to track fitness and nutrition goals.

Special Investigations Officer

What Does a Special Investigations Officer Do?

At a Glance:

Special Investigations Officer

Minimum Educational Requirements
College degree, preferably in criminology, criminal justice, or psychology

Personal Qualities
Critical thinker, problem solver, intelligent, adaptable

Working Conditions
Combat zones, offices, fieldwork, undercover

Salary Range
Monthly salary depends on pay grade and years of service

Future Outlook
Approximately 230 vacancies each year are filled by enlisted officers and law enforcement civilians

Special investigations officers (SIOs) have many duties, but all relate to studying possible criminal activity and protecting the military, or the country, against crime. As their title suggests, some of these officers are responsible for investigating major crimes involving Air Force personnel. These officers plan and conduct criminal investigations of people who are accused of violating federal laws whether in the physical world or in the virtual world of cyberspace.

During investigations these officers might search crime scenes for evidence, conduct surveillance operations, and organize line-ups of potential suspects. For example, in 2014 an investigation was conducted by SIOs when an airman was charged with attempted murder and arson. They searched the crime scene, interviewed witnesses, and reported that the airman had been stalking the target for some time and had acquired firearms and items needed to perpetrate arson. In this case the investigators helped convict a suspect, but in other instances they might uncover evidence to exonerate an accused individual.

SIOs are called in to examine evidence in a variety of crimes, including robbery, rape, assault, and drug trafficking. Despite working for the military, their job is not to protect service personnel who may be involved; instead, these officers remain unbiased, searching for the truth and helping ensure that justice is done. Investigating fraud is also part of the job. For instance, SIOs were able to recover more than $3.5 million from a company that sold the Air Force defective computer data storage devices that also jeopardized classified military information.

Since the Air Force aircraft fleet has the most advanced technology in the world, a unit of SIOs is assigned to safeguard confidential data and military information against criminal cyberactivity. Thus, protecting such valuable assets is another aspect of their duties. Similarly, some SIOs are specially trained to conduct counterintelligence missions involving known terrorist groups to keep their comrades and the nation safe. They deploy all over the world to gather information on foreign adversaries who are suspected of collecting and communicating confidential military intelligence and activities. In a Patrick Air Force Base online article, Special Agent Jason Canha attests to the diverse duties of this career by saying, "Yes, we are the ones who conduct felony level investigations, but we also conduct many other activities and operations that afford you the opportunity to live and work in a safe environment."

Sometimes creating a safe environment means taking the fight to those who threaten the safety of American forces and allies. In an Edwards Air Force Base online article, Special Agent Christopher Mitchell of the Office of Special Investigations describes his objectives during a deployment in Afghanistan: "We find, fix, track and neutralize terrorist threats in the area." During his deployment, Mitchell led more than one hundred attacks on enemy forces under extremely dangerous conditions. Additionally, he gathered critical information through a counterintelligence mission by recruiting active Taliban fighters who provided key information on attack commands and terrorist pockets. "What that involves is dealing with people directly, asking questions, and getting out and trying to figure out what the bad guys are up to," says Mitchell.

How Do You Become a Special Investigations Officer?

Education

Students who have an interest in this type of career would benefit from participation in the Air Force Junior Reserve Officers' Training Corps (AFJROTC). These students, called cadets, engage in curriculum that teaches leadership, team building, and physical conditioning. Additionally, many AFJROTC programs have special operations teams with cadets who are committed to fitness and academics through physical and mental conditioning. All members of the AFJROTC, however, are eligible to receive the Air Commando Association Award if they show excellence in the criteria needed for success: integrity, self-motivation, intelligence, self-discipline, perseverance, maturity, judgment, selflessness, leadership, physical fitness, adaptability, and family strength.

Even if a candidate possesses these attributes, entry into the special investigations specialization requires a bachelor's degree. However, this is a highly sought-after position in the Air Force, and applicants who have completed their degree in criminology, criminal justice, or psychology are often given preference when positions are available.

The initial training for all recruits from the Office of Special Investigations begins with the Criminal Investigator Training Program at the Air Force Special Investigations Academy. During this eleven-week course, instructors instruct trainees in investigative techniques, including search and seizure, interviewing informants, report writing, and testifying. They are also trained in firearms and defensive tactics. The course also involves coursework specific to the Office of Special Investigations organization, mission, and jurisdiction. Specific topics covered during this time prepare future officers in military law; property, civil, and environmental crime; counterintelligence; and fraud investigations. During this instruction trainees apply newly acquired skills to real-world situations, searching crime scenes, conducting surveillance, interviewing potential informants, and preparing an investigation report from activities documented during simulated experiences. In addition, to be fully certified as an SIO, trainees must pass the Physical Efficiency Battery, which consists of five physical fitness tests.

After completing training and serving in their new role for at least one year, many SIOs choose to continue their education with advanced coursework in surveillance detection, environmental crime investigations, digital forensics, and antiterrorism. Others are handpicked to attend a twelve-week advanced training course in technical surveillance countermeasures or a fourteen-week course on polygraph (lie detector) administration.

Skills and Personality

Because their job is to investigate criminal activity, SIOs need to be problem solvers and critical thinkers. Strong communication skills are important too. Good investigators also need to be open-minded, perceptive, and capable of asking probing questions. It takes a keen observer to accurately interpret and understand nonverbal reactions to questions and to separate fact from fiction.

They should also enjoy working independently since their job may require working for long hours in front of a computer going over details from a criminal investigation. However, investigators do compile evidence and testimony in teams. Being able to function as part of a group is essential because it is typically unrealistic to manage a case without the cooperation of forensic specialists and other professionals who bring their expertise to bear.

SIOs are also trained in taking notes and conducting interviews. It is important to keep an open mind during the interview process and during the writing of case reports. SIOs must take into account all sides of a case and then provide an unbiased report of the events. Being detail oriented and analytical are also crucial skills when writing a report that summarizes the facts of a case.

On the Job

Working Conditions

SIOs are given assignments to complete that often do not fall within a traditional nine-to-five workday. They can expect to work on an Air Force base, at a crime scene, or overseas gathering counterintelligence. They often collaborate with other government agencies, including the FBI, the Offices of the US Attorneys, and the Drug Enforcement Administration, while investigating cases of fraud, illegal drug use, and other criminal activities. This type of work often includes working undercover to gather information, interviewing informants, and working with victims of violent crimes.

In this profession, deployment happens frequently. For example, SIOs are often deployed overseas as part of intelligence-gathering operations involving terrorist groups. Aside from never knowing where they will be stationed, SIOs never know for sure what threats will arise in their host communities. Therefore, officers make a special effort to establish trust with community leaders. Special Agent Jack Muñoz and his team were stationed at the Tallil Air Base in Iraq. Their job was to work with local families, police officers, and vendors in an effort to stop enemies from collecting information on the base and to collect weapons in the community that might fall into the wrong hands. "We establish a personal relationship with these folks. We meet their families, have dinner with them and listen to their stories," Muñoz told the Air Force News Service. His team removed weapons from the hands of Iraqi children, got rid of unexploded ordnance in townspeople's backyards, and locked up explosives found in the community. "To have been able to take a lot of weapons off the streets that could have been used against us is extremely rewarding," Muñoz said. In addition, the Iraqis who benefited from the good deeds of the special investigations team were more inclined to pass on information about suspicious characters that might want to do harm to the Americans stationed there. That information helped protect the base and the community.

Earnings

Military pay is standardized and based on the member's pay grade and seniority. In addition to basic pay with automatic pay raises every one to two years, all enlisted members are eligible for supplemental payments and allowances, such as combat pay, flight pay, and food and housing allowances.

Opportunities for Advancement

When officers are eligible for a promotion, those who have earned the highest number of points are then advanced in rank. They earn points on the basis of factors such as time in the service and time in their current rank, awards and decorations, performance reports, education credits, and certifications. After completing the initial required coursework, advanced instruction is available to those officers who are interested in a more specialized training and advancement opportunities. For example, some officers receive advanced training in protective services. This area of expertise includes intercepting communications using video surveillance, tracing devices, phone tapping, and computer forensics. These SIOs are often promoted to personal security positions for senior military leaders while traveling to dangerous locations. Forensic science—which uses ultraviolet fingerprint detectors, digital photography, and digital blood analysis tools to analyze crime scenes—is another specialized field that officers might consider.

What Is the Future Outlook for a Special Investigations Officer?

The Air Force has openings for about 230 SIOs each year. It is the second most-requested career field in the Air Force. Because of its activities in investigating fraud in military supply contracting, the Office of Special Investigations has saved the government billions of dollars. Therefore, the Air Force has continued to keep this effective and cost-saving specialization open to interested applicants.

What Are Employment Prospects in the Civilian World?

SIOs have an excellent chance of transitioning into a civilian career in law enforcement or the intelligence community. Agencies such as the FBI, state or local police departments, Homeland Security, and the CIA find value in the experience of former SIOs and are often eager to recruit them.

There are also private military organizations and contractors that provide protection services and training programs. Because of their skills, experience, and training, SIOs are highly sought after for employment in these business sectors as well. For example, AT Solutions actively recruits those with experience in counterintelligence, global security, and weapons training for contract work with the federal government. Another private organization, the Chenega Corporation, offers the US government and private companies a variety of physical and cybersecurity protection services and training options that are run by ex-military personnel.

Pilot

What Does a Pilot Do?

Air Force pilots serve many different roles depending on the aircraft they are flying. They might transport food and equipment to troops deployed in combat zones, fly a tanker to the aid of another aircraft that needs refueling while in flight, or carry out a combat mission.

Fighter pilots fly combat aircraft such as the F-117A Nighthawk, the F-15 Eagle, and F-16 Fighting Falcon. Bomber pilots have the same responsibilities as fighter pilots but fly bomber aircraft, including the B-1B Lancer and the B-52 Stratofortress. Some of these pilots fly close support missions, aiding allied units on the ground; others may launch missiles or drop payloads of bombs from miles above their targets to disrupt enemy defenses or infrastructure.

Tanker pilots operate refueling aircraft and conduct airlift rescue missions. For example, pilot Joe Ratterree's duty includes flying a McDonnell Douglas KC-10 Extender that refuels other aircraft while in the air. In a 2013 interview for the *Making Strides* blog of the

---

At a Glance:

Pilot

Minimum Educational Requirements
College degree, preferably in aviation

Personal Qualities
Confident, decisive, intelligent, observant

Certification and Licensing
FAA pilot's license

Working Conditions
Combat zones and search-and-rescue operations

Salary Range
Monthly salary depends on pay grade and years of service

Number of Jobs
12,920 active-duty pilots

Future Outlook
Good, with bonuses being offered due to pilot shortages

A pilot preflights a C130-H Hercules cargo plane before embarking on her mission in Iraq. Depending on the aircraft, Air Force pilots have a variety of duties including flying combat missions, transporting cargo and personnel, and in-flight refueling of other aircraft.

educational travel company WorldStrides, Ratterree describes one mission in which his squadron refueled some stealth fighters on maneuvers. "My team and I created a formation of four KC-10s, which took off from McGuire Air Force Base [in New Jersey] and met six F-22s at a random point in space over the United States," he recalls. "And once we met the planes in mid-air, [the KC-10s] picked the six planes up [i.e., hooked up refueling hoses that kept them fueled] and took them all the way to Hawaii."

A select few Air Force pilots are also eligible to fly *Air Force One*, the aircraft that transports the president of the United States. Applicants must have clocked more than two thousand hours flying airlift, tanker, or combat aircraft and have international flight experience. *Air Force One* is a Boeing 747-200B jet that is specially equipped with an onboard medical facility, high-tech communication devices, and heavy shielding for aircraft protection.

All Air Force pilots have an important job to do. Whether they carry cargo or fuel, transport troops, or engage in combat, every mission takes many hours of on-ground planning. Pilots help in the planning by designing simulated practice or combat missions prior to carrying them out. They also have other on-ground responsibilities, including logging flight information, completing maintenance forms, and recording incidents. Captain Brian Boardman, a C-130J pilot interviewed for the Little Rock Air Force Base website, says that pilots only spend about 20 percent of their time in the air, with the rest of their time in preflight preparations such as gathering weather information, completing fuel calculations, and checking flight equipment. For Boardman, these duties do not match the excitement of being called to action. The Lockheed Martin C-130J Super Hercules four-engine turboprop military transportation craft serves multiple functions, so his job is never boring when he and his crew are airborne. "When we are in the aircraft, we are functioning at such a high intensity that time seems to go by at a faster pace than normal," says Boardman. "There are always opportunities to do something different, and experience something you have never done before. The days we are able to fly can be considered a 'break from the office,' a chance for us to go out and perform the core job we were all trained to do."

Pilots like Boardman recognize that their aircraft have multiple capabilities that might be needed at a moment's notice. Although performing training flights and practice missions are a way to keep pilots alert, all air personnel know that they could be called upon to conduct combat, rescue, or transport operations that have real-world consequences. Both the excitement and the challenge of those operations are what entice many Air Force cadets to become pilots.

How Do You Become a Pilot?

Physical Requirements

There are basic physical and health requirements for those interested in becoming a pilot. The aircraft have somewhat cramped cockpits; therefore, candidates must be between 5 feet 7 inches to 6 feet 5 inches (170 to 196 cm) tall when standing and 34 to 40 inches (86 to

102 cm) tall when sitting. They must also maintain a weight between 160 to 231 pounds (73 to 105 kg). Men cannot have more than 25 percent body fat and no more than 32 percent for women. Because pilots are expected to fly in a wide variety of weather conditions, in hostile airspace, and through a series of air maneuvers, they cannot be colorblind or have had laser-corrected vison. Applicants cannot have allergies or asthma because these conditions cause symptoms that impair a pilot's senses and may jeopardize flight operations.

Education

A limited number of positions are available each year for those interested in becoming an Air Force pilot. As a result, there is a lot of competition for each vacant spot. Getting an early start is key to getting noticed. Moriah Graham is a senior at Polytech High School in Woodside, Delaware, and a member of her school's Air Force Junior Reserve Officers' Training Corps (AFJROTC) program. She decided she wanted to be an Air Force pilot in seventh grade. During her junior year of high school, she began pilot training at Dover Air Force Base. She passed the Federal Aviation Administration's private pilot exam in May 2015, becoming the first African American young woman from Delaware to earn her pilot's license before graduating high school. Five other cadets at Polytech High School have used Graham as their role model, also earning their pilot's license during the same year. During a 2015 interview at Maxwell Air Force Base, Graham explained that she completed this training program not just for her pilot's license but also to serve as an inspiration to young African American girls, encouraging them to work hard and pursue their dreams.

In addition to flight preparation, Air Force pilots must obtain a bachelor's degree; however, the Air Force suggests earning that degree in aviation. This track provides a foundation in aerodynamics, piloting, meteorology, and flight training. Before enrolling in the officer training program or successfully completing the Air Force ROTC program at a participating four-year college, all potential officers must first successfully complete the Air Force Officer Qualifying Test (AFOQT). This five-hour, 380-question test measures knowledge and reasoning skills and is used as a placement tool in Officer

Training School. The test consists of math, aviation information and instrument comprehension, general sciences, and verbal analogies. To qualify for pilot training, candidates must also be able to read aircraft instruments and demonstrate knowledge of aeronautical concepts. After passing the AFOQT and completing Officer Training School (or completing the Air Force ROTC program), the next step is Undergraduate Pilot Training (UPT).

Phase one of UPT is four to six weeks of twelve-hour days of academic classes and preflight training. Coursework includes instruction on flight regulations, aerospace physiology, flight planning, and aviation weather. Trainees also log extensive hours on computer-based flight simulators called cockpit familiarization trainers. When trainees reach phase two, every day begins with a formal morning briefing in which the flight commander reviews key flight information such as weather, landing patterns, and emergency procedures. After the briefing, another twelve-hour day begins with flight practice in a trainer aircraft, simulation exercises, or studying in the flight room. Students work their way through phase two by earning daily grades that show they have mastered the given information or procedure. During the last phase of training, students choose either the fighter/bomber, airlift/tanker, helicopter, or turboprop track for their final training. This track allows students to train in a certain type of aircraft; it does not permit them to select a specific aircraft to fly. For example, all airlift/tanker track students will train in the T-1 Jayhawk. At the end of phase three, when UPT is complete, students then choose a specific aircraft for specialized training on the basis of their track.

Skills and Personality

Studies of Air Force pilots found that they scored highly on tests rating competitiveness and assertiveness. These are two qualities needed to operate aircraft in tense situations. Pilots often have to make quick decisions during air-based warfare or in difficult weather conditions. Thus, they have to be confident and decisive. Being able to keep calm, even in stressful situations, can make the difference between life and death. When a mission does not go according to plan, a pilot must make rational, on-the-spot decisions with precision. Much of their air time is spent responding to transmitted flying instructions and communicating back to other pilots or to controllers on the ground. Therefore, pilots need good communications skills.

Their job is to complete a mission safely and successfully. Pilots are sometimes required to navigate through hostile airspace or less-than-perfect weather conditions for hours at a time. This can be both mentally and physically demanding. Because of this, they are also required to meet some of the most rigorous physical fitness standards of all Air Force careers. A certain toughness of mind and body, then, are the traits that help make pilots used to the rigors of flying under extreme circumstances.

On the Job

Working Conditions

Pilots can be deployed to any Air Force base in the world. During their downtime, they might be found in an office filling out flight reports. However, when they are called upon—day or night—to pilot their aircraft, they remain in their cockpits until the mission is over. While in the air, a pilot might be expected to function normally during severe weather phenomena such as snowstorms and hurricanes. And, of course, if a pilot is participating in a combat situation, then he or she will be expected to function efficiently under stress.

Earnings

The Air Force has a standardized pay scale for officers based on rank, time in the military, and assigned duties. Most pilots begin their career at the pay scale rank of a first lieutenant, with the added benefit of free military base housing or a housing stipend. In addition, they are also given extra pay for each flight mission. A 2015 article in the *Air Force Times* reports that pilots who agree to serve an additional five years past their initial service commitment will be given a $125,000 bonus, or $25,000 each year. Those who extend an additional four years, nine years in total, will be given an additional $100,000 bonus. The Air Force is eager to keep its well-trained pilots because the skills they possess are needed every day in the service.

Opportunities for Advancement

An annual officer promotion is almost automatic for the first three years of service; however, the fourth rank, promotion to major (O-4), is more competitive. Pilots move beyond the initial ranks by passing a review process that examines performance, successful missions, and distinctions and honors earned.

What Is the Future Outlook for a Pilot?

Commercial airlines hire military pilots who have satisfied their commitment to the Air Force by offering large salaries and job security. Because this often draws qualified pilots away from the Air Force, the service is constantly seeking to fill pilot vacancies. According to the 2015 report of the Senate Committee on Armed Services, the Air Force is currently short 520 fighter pilots to meet the minimum level of combat readiness, with more vacant positions projected in the future. To overcome the high turnover rate, the Aviator Retention Program is designed to keep pilots active by offering signing and retention bonuses and other incentives. This makes the prospects good for those who might wish to make Air Force piloting a career.

What Are Employment Prospects in the Civilian World?

Commercial airlines and air cargo transport companies hire many former military pilots. Major commercial airlines are offering large salaries, health benefits, and job security to qualified pilots in order to fill their projected need of two thousand new positions every year until 2022. "I have just retired after 20 years of active duty as a fighter pilot, and have begun my second career with Delta Air Lines," a retired lieutenant colonel tells the *Air Force Times*. He explains that in addition to earning his retirement pension from the Air Force, his annual income will continue to increase with his new assignment. After five years with Delta, he expects to double his starting salary. Therefore, pilots who choose to leave the service can often walk into commercial jobs where their livelihoods are assured.

Pararescue Specialist

What Does a Pararescue Specialist Do?

Pararescue specialists are also known as pararescue jumpers (PJs) or as parajumpers. As their motto—"These things we do, that others may live"—implies, these airmen are highly trained emergency medical technicians with combat and survival skills. Currently, the Air Force only permits men to serve on pararescue teams.

Deployed throughout the world on lifesaving missions, a PJ's job is to safely rescue soldiers who are difficult to reach—either because of combat, terrain, or weather. Although some missions are carefully planned ahead of time, most often pararescue specialists are deployed without warning and may be called upon to perform multiple duties. In 2012 Technical Sergeant Daniel Warren was enjoying some much-needed sleep on his night off when he was called into action. He explains on Pararescue.com that only a short time later he was at the tactical operations center gearing up with night-vision goggles and a

At a Glance:
Pararescue Specialist

Minimum Educational Requirements
High school diploma or GED

Personal Qualities
Self-disciplined, adaptable, flexible, able to make personal sacrifices

Certification and Licensing
Paramedic certification

Working Conditions
Combat zones, search-and-rescue missions, humanitarian aid

Salary Range
Monthly salary depends on pay grade and years of service

Number of Jobs
170 active-duty airmen serve in pararescue

Future Outlook
Signing bonuses and an increase in funding suggest good future outlook

rifle. From there he flew directly to Camp Bastion in Afghanistan to aid fellow soldiers. He and two other pararescue specialists ended up fighting off insurgents bent on attacking the base. For this action, he was awarded the Bronze Star. "Our whole mission is to save lives where very few people can," Warren humbly explained to the Reminder, an Internet news site. Training for rescue but also anticipating the possibility of battling enemies is what makes pararescue specialists unique.

On location with its camera crew, the National Geographic Channel investigated the job of a pararescue specialist for a 2013 series called *Inside Combat Rescue.* The series began by stating that since the September 11, 2001, terrorist attacks, PJs have conducted more than twelve thousand lifesaving missions on the battlefield and five thousand civilian rescue missions. During filming, camera crews witnessed rescue missions that included hanging from an aircraft cable amidst enemy fire, stabilizing injuries during a mountainside rescue, and recovering live explosives off the coast of Africa. The diversity of missions exemplifies how pararescue personnel are utilized to help save lives in all environments.

How Do You Become a Pararescue Specialist?

Physical Requirements

Pararescue specialists must have vision that can be corrected to 20/20, be between 5 feet and 6 feet 5 inches (152 to 196 cm) tall, and weigh no more than 250 pounds (113 kg). Before beginning basic training, candidates must successfully complete each element of the Physical Ability and Stamina Test. In a three-hour time limit, candidates must swim underwater for 20 meters (66 ft), freestyle swim for 500 meters (547 yd), and run for 1.5 miles (2.4 km). In addition, candidates must complete as many chin-ups, flutter kicks, push-ups, and sit-ups as possible within one or two minutes for each exercise. The Air Force Special Operations Command online newsletter interviewed eighteen candidates about their experiences while taking the test. Adam Small was taking the test again to improve his score even though he was already accepted into the basic training program. He explained, "When I first started . . . , I couldn't even swim one lap across the pool, so I just jumped in the pool and started training." After one month, he was swimming five laps; then, after only three months, he could swim a mile. His advice to those who do not pass the first time around is "don't give up."

Education

Candidates for pararescue operations must have a high school diploma and earn a minimum specific score on the Armed Services Vocational Aptitude Battery (ASVAB) exam. However, to prepare for this physically and mentally challenging position in the Air Force, training needs to begin early. The Air Force Junior Reserve Officers' Training Corps (AFJROTC) teaches high school students self-discipline and a sense of responsibility. It also promotes community service, which encourages selflessness and duty to country. Every AFJROTC has a Cadet Health/Wellness Program component that helps cadets improve their physical fitness through running, calisthenics, and other exercises. Many of these programs have preparation training that helps cadets through the physical conditioning required of all special operations officers, including pararescue specialists.

After completing eight weeks of basic training, a career in special operations takes an additional two years of preparation through course- and fieldwork. Candidate school is ten weeks of team training with an emphasis on physical endurance. During this training students will also be exposed to academic instruction on weapons, CPR, leadership and team building, medical and dive terminology, and dive physics. After this, candidates can follow the pipeline to become a pararescue specialist. Every day includes rigorous cardiovascular, endurance, and underwater training. There also is the three-week Basic Airborne Course that provides training on military parachuting skills. This course teaches students how to safely drop from an aircraft, land on the ground, and advance to the target combat zone. After this course, students progress to the four-week Combat Diver Course. They learn to navigate through tactical environments 130 feet (40 m) underwater while using closed-circuit diving equipment and scuba gear. A one-day Underwater Egress Training follows, teaching how to escape from a sinking aircraft. The next course, Basic Survival School, exposes students to important survival skills in secluded and

A crew member hoists a two-man pararescue team into an HH-60 Pave Hawk helicopter during a training exercise. Air Force pararescue specialists deploy throughout the world on missions to rescue captured US and allied military personnel.

unfriendly environments so they can uphold the training motto, Return with Honor. The next five weeks are spent at the Military Freefall Parachutist School, where advanced parachuting techniques are learned. The course includes classroom instruction, practice, and actual parachuting operations to teach students wind-tunneling training, aerial maneuvers, and parachute-opening procedures.

Administering emergency medical treatment and dealing with life-threatening trauma is an essential part of every pararescueman's job. The next phase of training is the twenty-two-week Paramedic Course, which culminates with the candidate becoming a nationally certified paramedic. The final twenty-four weeks of training are spent in the Pararescue Recovery Specialist Course. The last training in the pararescue pipeline includes field and combat tactics, advanced parachuting and helicopter rescues, and field medical care. Successfully completing this final course qualifies pararescuers for active duty and deployment anywhere in the world.

Skills and Personality

Personal sacrifice and self-discipline are the learned skills for pararescue specialists. These traits go hand in hand with adaptability and flexibility, as these specialists may be called to duty any time of day, in any environment, anywhere in the world. Because pararescue missions can involve traversing the desert, scuba diving 130 feet (40 m) into dangerous waters, or rescuing flood victims from a helicopter, physical fitness is mandatory. Pararescue specialists are often called upon to push their bodies to complete their duties, so physical toughness is a key attribute. In addition, most rescues are carried out by a team, so knowing how to work as part of a team is also essential. This never-quit mindset is what carries pararescue specialists through all challenging rescue operations.

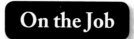

Working Conditions

Whatever it takes and wherever it takes them, the mission of pararescue is to rescue, recover, and return. On call twenty-four hours a day, they are prepared to deploy for search-and-rescue missions in both friendly and hostile environments on land, air, and sea. Climate, terrain, and enemy fire must be braved in order for pararescuers to accomplish their missions. One CNN reporter describes the pararescue job as "a kind of cross between a Green Beret and an emergency trauma paramedic." In the CNN article, a pararescue specialist working in Iraq and Afghanistan notes that his team has to be ready for more than just rescuing the injured. "Insurgents have laid ambushes, or placed bombs or other 'secondary devices,' that specifically target the rescue teams. They call these 'SAR traps,' short for Search and Rescue traps." Such devices have claimed the lives of several rescuers in Iraq and Afghanistan, but the pararescuers continue to deal with the hazards in an effort to bring home injured comrades. As another specialist in the article attests, "If you're out there, we'll go get you."

Earnings

In addition to being based on rank and time in service, pararescue specialist pay is supplemented by hazard pay and bonuses for conducting missions. Pararescuers can also earn additional income for dive pay, flight pay, parachutist pay, and special duty incentive pay. As with all enlisted military, additional incentives include free housing and medical and dental care.

Opportunities for Advancement

Officer promotions are based on a board review system. An annual officer promotion is almost automatic for the first three years; however, the fourth rank promotion to major (O-4) is more competitive. Promotion to the higher ranks involves earning distinctions and honors, participating in successful missions, and otherwise standing out from one's peers.

What Is the Future Outlook for a Pararescue Specialist?

Currently there is a shortage of pararescue specialists. Of the 200 positions offered yearly, only about 170 are routinely filled. In addition, the *National Defense* online magazine reports that those who serve under the special operations command (which includes pararescue personnel) are seeing an increase in funding, and that means more opportunities for signing and retention bonuses.

What Are Employment Prospects in the Civilian World?

The skills pararescue specialists acquire during their time in the Air Force is transferable to multiple career fields in the civilian world. With background expertise in emergency medical rescue and care, a pararescuer can go on to pursue a career as a paramedic or an in-flight paramedic. For those individuals who are interested in pursuing a medical degree, many pararescue specialists use their GI Bill funds to continue their education. The Pararescue Doctor Association was set up to provide information and assist with the application process all the way through residency for pararescuers interested in attending medical school.

Some former pararescue personnel turn their special operations training into other types of business ventures. For example, Tactivate and the Peak are two companies that provide wilderness training, team building, and outdoor adventures for individuals, groups, and companies. Retired pararescue chief master sergeant Rod Alne and Air Force veteran and neurosurgeon Gus Varavas, started the Peak, a training and consulting firm that caters to individuals and companies interested in backcountry travel, climbing and rope rescue, and wilderness medicine. The company offers more advanced training to law enforcement and military organizations, including parachute, diving, and pack animal operation training. Groups can also schedule tailored leadership and team-building adventures. In addition, Alne and Varavas have a side job evaluating the effectiveness of wilderness equipment and products sold to the public.

Private consulting is another option for those with entrepreneurial spirit. At X-G Productions, retired pararescue team leader Ken Fournier offers consultation services, technical advisement, and stunt training to media producers who want to add authenticity to their television programs, films, and video games. According to the company's website, Fournier and his staff, who also have military backgrounds, provide "on-set/on-location law enforcement and military technical expertise regarding tactical operations, gun handling, handcuffing, arrest skills, SWAT operations, airborne operations, and counter insurgency, hostage rescue, hostage negotiations, profiling, interviewing, etc." They rely on their own experiences to teach others how such events and procedures would play out in real-world situations that few other people have encountered.

Weather Officer

What Does a Weather Officer Do?

Knowing the weather both on the ground and in the air is crucial for planning operations. Air missions depend on clear visibility, and ground maneuvers are easier to conduct when it is not raining or snowing. The Air Force's weather service provides weather and space forecasting to the military, the Department of Defense, and other government agencies. It is the most important source of global weather data used for staging tactical combat operations. Therefore, weather officers are an essential part of the Air Force.

It is the job of the Air Force Weather Agency and its weather officers to make sure that mission planners have accurate, up-to-date weather information when they need it. Meteorological weather information is predicted using satellites, radar, weather balloons, and even thermometers. All of the collected feedback is then fed into supercomputers. The data is interpreted by advanced software that provides an atmospheric weather forecast. This information is used to predict weather changes that might affect ground

At a Glance:
Weather Officer

Minimum Educational Requirements
College degree, preferably in meteorology, atmospheric science, or space and weather science

Personal Qualities
Strong communication skills, organized

Working Conditions
Combat zones, weather stations, observatories

Salary Range
Monthly salary depends on pay grade and years of service

Number of Jobs
Approximately 4,100 active-duty, reserve, and civilian jobs

Future Outlook
Signing bonuses suggest good future outlook

missions and underwater operations, but it is also important for determining whether aircraft can perform at all. In an interview with the Barksdale Air Force Base online news service, Senior Airman Gary Graeff explains that "having accurate, up-to-date weather information is of vital importance to the Air Force since it directly affects an aircraft's ability to fly safely. Each time a plane's aircrew is scheduled to leave the ground, for training or otherwise, leadership must take the weather into account and weigh the risks." Whereas ground forces, for example, can still function in poor weather conditions, airplanes are often grounded if the weather makes it dangerous to fly or otherwise impairs the capabilities of the onboard systems.

In addition to interpreting weather data, weather officers are responsible for conducting meteorological and space research aimed at improving forecasting. This work involves analyzing how terrestrial and nonterrestrial forces impact weather. For example, they may conduct research into how Earth's magnetic field impacts weather patterns. Their findings are often used to improve instruments and technologies that military planners rely on for training and combat missions. Sergeant Susan Dickson is a solar analyst with the space weather squadron that runs the Air Force's Ramey Solar Observatory in Aguadilla, Puerto Rico. This observatory is one of six worldwide where other space weather squadrons are stationed. Ramey airmen are part of a global network that monitors solar flares that may cause space, air, and ocean craft to have communication problems due to an overload of electromagnetic waves. Master Sergeant Bob Silvernail, a solar analyst who works with Sergeant Dickson, explains in an online article on About.com that "knowing what's coming and when allows the military to change operations so solar energy bursts won't have such an impact. And all fixes to overcome solar flare interference aren't rocket science."

How Do You Become a Weather Officer?

Education

Some Air Force Junior Reserve Officers' Training Corps (AFJROTC) programs have approved course lists that include classes

An Air Force aerial reconnaissance weather officer analyzes meteorological and atmospheric conditions during a tropical storm. Military ground and air operations depend on accurate weather and climate information.

focusing on weather and flight conditions. Norwin High School in North Huntingdon, Pennsylvania, for example, offers the Working Through Flight Conditions Course. Cadets explore how weather conditions impact flights by analyzing atmospheric conditions, cloud types, and pressure systems. The AFJROTC program in the Jackson County School District in Mississippi has an entire extracurricular Air Force Weather Agency program to help cadets understand the importance of weather in aircraft safety. To further prepare for a job as a weather officer, high school students should also take courses in physics, chemistry, earth sciences, and advanced math classes.

Before becoming an officer with a weather specialization, an enlistee must earn a four-year college degree with a minimum of twenty-four semester hours in meteorology courses such as dynamic meteorology and analysis and prediction of weather systems. Preference is given to those with a degree in meteorology, atmospheric science, or space and weather science.

Those interested in obtaining an officer rank must also complete Officer Training School and then pass through the Weather Officer Initial Skills Course. New officers will learn about weather support and chart analysis, satellite imagery interpretation, oceanography, and automated weather distribution systems. Additional coursework is offered for those seeking to progress through the field or into more-focused specializations. For example, candidates interested in working with a weather flight unit or with the Army's weather support units should take the Advanced Weather Exploitation and Integration Course. This course provides advanced information on tactical weather support, which helps with making weather-based decisions on conducting warfare operations. After advanced courses are taken, most weather officers will begin their career in an operational weather squadron for at least a year. During that time, they will put training into practice on all aspects of Air Force meteorology, such as tactical forecasting, predicting atmospheric changes, and decoding satellite weather messages.

After successfully completing the initial training course, a weather officer might be interested in joining the special operations team. These officers learn weather skills but also are trained in combat. They are rigorously trained in physical fitness to meet the demands of special operations. Their mission is to be inserted into dangerous regions or difficult terrain to gather meteorological data that can impact operations in those areas. This new path begins with the two-week Special Operations Weather Selection Course and then twenty-nine weeks in the Special Operations Weather Initial Skills Course. Another three weeks in basic airborne training is necessary to learn the skills needed for jumps into hostile or challenging locales. The final program ends with the thirteen-week Special Operations Weather Apprentice Course. Special operations weather technician (SOWT) officers "don't just do the weather. They leverage it," writes Tony Dokoupil for NBC news online. He explains that they use the weather as an opportunity; the noise of high wind predictions to hide the sound of an Air Force helicopter, and take advantage of heavy fog to wipe out foot traffic into hostile territory. They also look for favorable circumstances to create obstacles for enemies, such as soft soil, loose snow, or fast-running waters. In the same article, Jonathan Swatelle, an SOWT officer, says, "We live out our forecasts. . . . We're sensors, human sensors, and that's the magic of the SOWTs."

Volunteer Work and Internships

Students who attend schools that have WeatherSTEM or other on-line climate forecasting programs can gain meteorological experience by participating in these activities. WeatherSTEM is a curriculum that is driven by a live data feed from school-based or home-based instruments. Students can also take part in science, technology, engineering, and math (STEM) outreach programs. In one such program, students and teachers volunteered at Vandenberg Air Force Base to participate in a satellite launch.

Skills and Personality

No matter what their specialty, weather officers must have good communication and organizational skills and a strong background in science and math. Weather officers also need to have an aptitude for using complex instruments and for data analysis and interpretation. Technical Sergeant Gregory Spiker, a meteorology and oceanography operations weather forecaster at Camp Lemonnier in Djibouti, Africa, embodies the character traits required of a weather officer. In a Department of Defense online article, Spiker's squadron supervisor describes him as "energetic, motivated and very involved with the fighter squadrons here and what we do on the weather side. He's positive, has a good attitude and is a stellar NCO [noncommissioned officer]." If Spiker decides to seek an officer commission, he would have the skills and personality needed to succeed as he furthered his career.

On the Job

Working Conditions

Working conditions vary depending on the weather officer's chosen career path. Some weather officers work in offices or in observatories located at US or overseas bases. They may spend their days in front of computers or working on meteorological equipment outdoors. Others work on the battlefield, using portable devices or specially designed vehicles to gather and relay weather data to central commands. Special operations weather officers join their teams in conducting dangerous maneuvers in hostile environments.

Earnings

The military has a standardized pay scale based on factors such as years of service and time in rank. However, the Air Force has identified seventeen high-need careers that are undermanned, including weather officer. These positions are eligible for signing and education bonuses, extra paid vacation, and other incentives to attract qualified personnel.

Opportunities for Advancement

Promotions in the Air Force are based on a board review system. To be eligible for a promotion, officers must prove a history of positive evaluations and show strong performances in challenging assignments. Completing professional military education courses is another way to establish a record of excellence.

Those who are just beginning their weather career typically work as operational forecasters. Operational forecasters report on weather conditions over the past twenty-four hours. As they gain more experience and knowledge of all aspects of Air Force weather forecasting and meteorology, they are given more responsibilities and may help coordinate battlefield operations. Weather officer staff sergeant Logan English knows how important his job is to the soldiers in the field. In an online news article for *Airman* magazine, he states, "We're constantly evaluating conditions and our expertise is needed in the tactical operations center (TOC) and planning sections to ensure we don't send people out into bad situations." During his deployment in Afghanistan, English was responsible for accurately assessing weather conditions for over 11,000 square miles (28,490 sq km) of mountainous terrain where planes and ground forces operated.

Those who are interested in advancing their careers to special operations can continue their training and education to become special operations weather officers. They conduct reconnaissance missions on land, on the sea, and in the air. Their job is to observe, collect, and analyze climate information in hostile areas for use in the planning of missions. Moving into this specialization, though, requires additional physical conditioning and special operations training.

What Is the Future Outlook for a Weather Officer?

The Air Force Weather Agency has a $175 million budget that includes money to purchase new equipment and provide upgraded training and certifications. Because the agency is critically understaffed, the budget also provides for signing bonuses for those interested in pursuing a career in weather. All of this suggests a good future outlook for weather officers.

What Are Employment Prospects in the Civilian World?

After leaving the service, a former weather officer might find civilian work in weather forecasting for either government or private agencies. For example, the National Weather Service hires meteorologists who are retired military weather officers because they have the requisite expertise. Some former weather officers might seek opportunities with commercial airlines that need forecasters for planning safe travel routes. Another option is private consulting. Retired lieutenant colonel John Shewchuk, for example, provides expert testimony as a forensic meteorologist in legal matters in which weather was a factor. The variety of opportunities is great, but all rely on the individual possessing the technological skills and years of training needed to interpret and convey weather information. The Air Force provides this type of background, so former weather officers often can make the transition more easily.

Cybersystems Operations Specialist

At a Glance:
Cybersystems Operations Specialist

Minimum Educational Requirements
High school diploma or GED

Personal Qualities
Problem solver, meticulous, detail oriented, able to work independently and at a computer for long stretches

Certification and Licensing
CompTIA certification

Working Conditions
Typically in office settings; some combat-ready personnel are deployed on battlefields

Salary Range
Monthly salary depends on pay grade and years of service

Future Outlook
Good; about 1,700 new positions planned in 2016

What Does a Cybersystems Operations Specialist Do?

The Air Force has a history of conducting missions in the air, on land, in the water, and in space. As technology advances, it is now adding cyberspace to this list. Yet it is different from all the other domains because it is human-made. This new territory includes the Internet, computer systems, communication networks, and the information that is transmitted across these platforms. The Air Force depends on its cyberspecialists to design and create an entire cyberoperations system that links air, space, land, and maritime operations to a reliable cybernetwork of communication. They are also responsible for everyday electronic communications that many people take for granted, such as e-mail, Internet support, and protection against computer viruses. In an online newsletter out of Osan Air Base in South Korea, Major Scott Jensen of the Fifty-First Communications Squadron in cybersystems operations explains, "We are data transport providers—everything from airfield systems, weather systems and radar, to e-mail and server security. . . . Basically, if there's a way to send a message from 'point A' to 'point B' we handle it."

Cybersystems are integrated into planning and coordinating Air Force missions. They are also used during tactical operations to communicate combat strategies, arrange air strikes, and handle emergency situations. For this reason, cybersystems operations specialists (COSs) are a critical part of military efforts. These men and women make sure that data is transmitted quickly and accurately, but they also keep the network of communication secure from outsiders. Major Dave Neuman, who is in charge of the Ninety-Second Information Operations Squadron, explained in a 2012 online news story that the Air Force is constantly updating and reinforcing, or "hardening," its cybersystems and operations against the growing threat of cyberattacks. "If you look at it like a house, hardening is about locking the doors and windows so bad guys can't get in," Neuman stated. "Defending is more like using physical force in order to repel those bad guys." Since military sites in cyberspace cannot be defended, they must be made secure, and that is one of the main jobs of the COS.

COSs also design, install, and support digital systems. In addition to making them safe from hacking and cybercrimes, COSs make sure that the channels of communication between these devices are always fully operational. They also operate, monitor, and update critical software systems that keep Air Force computer systems up and running. During a power or network outage, these professionals make sure that a contingency plan is in place that will recover important data and maintain essential mission information.

COSs are problem solvers. Their job is vital to the overall success of every mission because they have to figure out the tactical and strategic cyberoperations system needed. This includes the devices that will need to be transported, the software that will need to be installed, and the means to build a secure network considering the mission's location. Not only do they make sure that enemies cannot intercept communications, they also must figure out the quickest way to relay electronic information to get the job done.

Some COSs deploy with soldiers on the battlefield. Those working under a combat communications group, for example, ensure that a strong communication network connects all levels of command. These specialists set up base-level communication equipment, ready encrypted high-speed data transmissions, and maintain a reliable power supply for telecommunications. They know that effective communication means an effective combat mission. An article on the Twenty-Fourth Air Force's website describes how this team's job impacts the lives of everyone on the base. Master Sergeant Rodney Norman points out that in addition to food, fuel, and water, a base needs reliable communication devices to be fully functional, including satellite and network equipment, computers, phones, and radios.

How Do You Become a Cybersystems Operations Specialist?

Education

Entry into this specialty requires a high school diploma or the equivalent and a score of at least 64 in the general section of the Armed Services Vocational Aptitude Battery (ASVAB) exam. Taking courses in science, technology, engineering, and math (STEM) will provide students with a foundation for this career. The Air Force has a STEM outreach program and offers activities on its bases throughout the country. For example, Vandenberg Air Force Base in California hosts rocketry, robotics, and basic engineering programs for high school students, and the Wright-Patterson Air Force Base in Ohio provides activities in aviation, aerospace, and science. All focus on the use of computers and technology in analyzing data or making things work.

After enlisting and completing basic training, COSs are immersed in the basics of computer network design and maintenance. Their objective is to earn a Computer Technology Industry Association (CompTIA) certificate by passing three courses over nine weeks. Training at Kessler Air Force Base in Mississippi begins with the

Information Technology Fundamentals Course, which lays a foundation in information technology, the Windows operating system, and Air Force cybersystems. The next course, which involves becoming a cybersystems operations apprentice, is six weeks long. COS students learn about how to identify and repair defective computer and network components that may cause a breach in cybersecurity or interfere with communications. They are also taught the basics of the Air Force network and the database system. The final two-week course reviews the job duties and responsibilities of a COS.

Volunteer Work and Internships

High school students who have an interest in cybersystems operations should take computer science and pre-engineering classes either at school or through a community outreach program. This will provide a background in computer hardware and software as well as an introduction to the significance of computers in today's society. The Air Force knows how important cybersystems operations are to keeping the country safe from cyberattacks and cybercrimes. It has developed partnerships with outside organizations to encourage students to consider a military career in aerospace cybersecurity or STEM. One such partnership is the National Youth Cyber Education Program, known as CyberPatriot. This program hosts the National Youth Cyber Defense Competition in which teams of middle and high school students are tasked with managing the network of a pretend company. They are challenged to find and fix cybersecurity flaws to get their simulated operating system up and running. The teams begin at the state level with opportunities to win a trip to Washington, DC, for the National Finals Competition. Winners can earn national recognition and scholarships.

Skills and Personality

The typical COS is a problem solver—someone who can spend hours at a time in front of a computer while fixing a glitch or finding a solution to a nagging issue. COSs must be meticulous and detail oriented. They need to be computer savvy and have an aptitude for working with the latest technology. This job also requires being able to stay calm and focused under pressure. Setting up a full communications system in a combat zone can be a stressful situation. It has to be in full working order as quickly as possible, and often in the middle of nowhere.

Not surprisingly, COSs typically love technology and computers. Having a knack for computer programming or at least a familiarity with the uses and capabilities of computers can help potential specialists quickly adjust to the demands of the job. Because COSs spend long hours in front of computers or wiring networks, individuals who are used to that kind of activity might find the duties less taxing.

On the Job

Working Conditions

COSs can be stationed at military facilities anywhere around the world. They are often in an office setting in front of a computer or a bank of computers, but those who work for a combat communications group are prepared to deploy to the battlefield at any time. The Fifth Combat Communications Group, for example, helped set up communications networks in Iraq that were designed to keep communications open while the country transitioned to a stable government. In an article on the Air Force Space Command website, Staff Sergeant Mike Meares describes the battlefield conditions faced by this unit and others like it. "Combat communicators are normally one of the first teams to enter an area of operations to lay down initial tactical communications capabilities," Meares states. "They typically operate autonomously, setting up their own amenities in austere locations." Therefore, those interested in becoming a COS may find some choice in what capacity and environment—in the field or on a base— they wish to work.

Earnings

COSs follow along the Air Force's standardized pay scale. They are also provided free or discount housing and medical and dental care.

Opportunities for Advancement

COSs begin their careers as apprentices, with the rank of airman first class. Through the Weighted Airman Promotion System, they are eligible for promotion to senior airman by earning points in supervision and leadership skills, through performance evaluations, and by completing the Career Development Course to become a journeyman. Being promoted to the next level of staff sergeant requires at least three years in service and completion of the Airman Leadership School. As they rise in rank, it is more difficult for specialists to advance because of fewer vacancies and increased competition.

Beginning at the apprentice level, COSs are eligible for jobs such as troubleshooting and repairing operating systems or developing computer programs that advance technology warfare. Being promoted through the ranks means gaining more supervisory and management positions such as shift leader responsibilities. Supervisors may be in charge of a detail of cybersystem operators, but the responsibility for completing missions is entirely on the supervisor.

What Is the Future Outlook for Cybersystems Operations Specialists?

The future for COSs is good. US Cyber Command (USCYBER-COM)—a command made up of service personnel from different branches of the military—is looking to increase its staff by employing qualified operations specialists. To meet 2016 quotas, USCYBER-COM was seeking 1,715 Air Force personnel to fill Cyber Mission Force teams that will be in charge of specific cyberspace operations and military networks. USCYBERCOM has been offering bonuses to applicants with sought-after skills.

What Are Employment Prospects in the Civilian World?

Computer specialists, especially those with experience in cybersecurity, are more in demand than ever before. After leaving the Air Force, COSs will find many job opportunities in the civilian information technology industry. Salaries for people with a certified information systems security professional certification range from $72,000 to $147,000 per year, according to the Academy of Computer Education, a professional computer training organization. According to the CompTIA certification webpage, companies such as Apple, Canon, Dell, and Toshiba, as well as the Department of Defense and other government agencies, are all hiring people with cybersecurity experience. Former military personnel who had security clearance are also in demand.

Crew Chief

What Does a Crew Chief Do?

Crew chiefs have a big responsibility. They are charged with the care and maintenance of the Air Force's multimillion-dollar jets. Crew chiefs are on the flight line when planes take off and land, directing the maintenance crews detailed to each plane. Pilots have to focus on navigating the aircraft and successfully completing their mission. Worrying about the aircraft's nosecone-to-tail maintenance and flight readiness is left to the crew chiefs. Troy Altevers, a crew chief production superintendent who began his twenty-year Air Force career as a crew chief apprentice, told the author during a phone interview that after he is assigned to an F-15 fighter, "I put my name on my jet. It's my jet and my responsibility."

Crew chiefs are responsible for performing all preflight through postflight aircraft service. They evaluate each system on board the aircraft, including the hydraulics, electrical, navigation, and flight control systems. Crew chiefs use computers to generate a diagnostic report of the aircraft's overall health. This report is used to identify maintenance problems,

At a Glance:
Crew Chief

Minimum Educational Requirements
High school diploma or GED

Personal Qualities
Self-confidence, discipline, team player, hard worker

Working Conditions
On the flight line at air bases

Salary Range
Monthly salary depends on pay grade and years of service

Number of Jobs
As of 2011, there were 49,237 active-duty mechanics, including crew chiefs

Future Outlook
8 to 14 percent job growth through 2022

electrical shortages, and malfunctions in the aircraft's technology system. Although crew chiefs are responsible for the general maintenance and repairs of their assigned aircraft, they also coordinate with specialists if there is problem with an advanced system, such as avionics or propulsion. One system malfunction may impact the entire aircraft and jeopardize the flight.

A crew chief's job is not easy. Sometimes it takes two crew chiefs to manage a single aircraft. For example, two chiefs work on the $60 million Lockheed U-2 reconnaissance jet stationed at Osan Air Base in South Korea. The jet is responsible for sending images during conflict situations. One crew chief prepares the jet for launch, and the other is assigned to recovery and inspection after the craft returns. "The preparation and launch shift begins the launch preparation approximately five hours prior to takeoff," explains Tech Sergeant Christopher Trusnik in an article on the Beale Air Force Base website. The recovery and inspection crew sets up tools about thirty minutes before the jet lands. After landing, the second crew chief takes over. "The crew chiefs then perform a post-flight inspection at the end of the flying day to ensure the aircraft will be structurally fit for its next flight as well as that all fluids and lubricants are at a sufficient level," the article explains. "I have worked on this aircraft my whole career, and I love it," Trusnik adds. "It is very satisfying to watch the aircraft take off after we have sunk more than 12 hours into repairing it to meet each mission requirement."

No matter where they are stationed or the aircraft assignment, crew chiefs are dedicated to the job and honored to contribute to the Air Force's flight. At the end of the day, the crew chiefs can proudly say that it was their jet that saved lives, successfully completed a mission, or awed crowds at an air show.

How Do You Become Crew Chief?

Education

To enter this field, candidates must have a high school diploma or its equivalent and score at least 47 in the mechanical section of the Armed Services Vocational Aptitude Battery (ASVAB). The Air

Two crew chiefs prepare a B-1B Lancer for combat operations in the Middle East. Air Force crew chiefs are responsible for the care and maintenance of aircraft, including all preflight through postflight service.

Force recommends prior experience in aircraft maintenance, repair, or engineering before enlisting. Many high schools offer science, technology, engineering, and math programs that provide students with a strong math and science background, which is needed when servicing tactical aircraft. Joining the Air Force Junior Reserve Officers' Training Corps in high school provides a foundation in leadership, self-confidence, and discipline. Current and retired crew chiefs have identified all of these skills as valuable to career success.

Before training as a crew chief, newly enlisted airmen must successfully complete basic training, which is followed by four months of classroom instruction and hands-on training in tactical aircraft maintenance. Keeping pilots in the air can only happen when crew chiefs are also trained on aircraft systems, including electrical, cooling, and communications. Even though the Air Force has hydraulic system specialists, crew chiefs also learn the basics of this system to assess the aircraft's landing gear and brakes.

After completing the tactical aircraft technical training, crew chiefs are assigned to a specific type of aircraft—such as a fighter jet, tanker, cargo, or reconnaissance plane—to learn the basics. Then crew chiefs are assigned their own aircraft, and on-the-job training begins. This assignment determines the Air Force base where the training will take place and how long it will last. At Luke Air Force Base in Arizona, crew chiefs learn to work on one of the most technologically advanced aircraft in the fleet: the F-16 Fighting Falcon. Here, the mission-ready airman training program for crew chiefs covers aircraft inspections, launch and recovery, and aircraft servicing of the F-16. The first seventeen days of training are conducted on the flight line. Only three days are spent in a classroom.

Students who are assigned to the F-35 Lightning II are stationed at Eglin Air Force Base in Florida. At Eglin, crew chiefs are typically trained on aircraft simulators. In a 2014 news article on the Eglin Air Force Base website, Staff Sergeant Ralph Davis, a crew chief instructor, explained that training for these cutting-edge jets are almost all computer-based learning modules. When inexperienced airman arrive for training, they can quickly learn how to perform complex maintenance tasks. Trevor Taylor, another instructor and staff sergeant interviewed for the article, looked back on his own crew chief training: "The majority of my F-15 training took place in a classroom where most of the hands-on training was performed on props, models or older block versions of aircraft." In contrast, Taylor noted that today's "airmen get to work on the current aircraft itself or simulators that closely mirror operational aircraft."

Volunteer Work and Internships

Those interested in becoming a crew chief should have an interest in working on a team that spends most of its time doing hands-on construction or maintenance. Volunteering to build sets for a school's drama department is a great place to practice team building, construction, and working in a fast-paced environment. Taking coursework in computer science will bolster the technical side needed to begin assessing the many high-tech systems on aircraft. However, assisting in hands-on mechanical work of any type will give interested individuals an idea of the physical demands of the job.

Skills and Personality

Crew chiefs have earned a reputation in the Air Force for being cocky. They know their job is important; without them, pilots could not do their jobs. They are the last people to touch a jet before it is cleared for takeoff and the first to inspect it after landing. On the *Air Force Live* blog, Staff Sergeant James McFadden, who has been a crew chief for twenty years, comments that "every good crew chief knows how important they are," even if they don't talk about it.

Work as a crew chief is anything but boring. Variety and spontaneity mark this job, and crew chiefs realize that the routine of maintenance goes hand in hand with the surprise of finding and fixing a specific malfunction. If there is a last-minute problem keeping a plane from flying, its crew chief must work quickly to solve the issue and get the aircraft off the ground. This kind of responsibility requires someone who works well in stressful situations. Crew chiefs do not solve problems alone, however, so being part of a team is another essential characteristic.

Working Conditions

Crew chiefs work on bases all over the world. When a pilot is deployed overseas, there is a good chance the crew chief will also be deployed to maintain and repair the pilot's aircraft. Being on call twenty-four hours a day, seven days a week to service a single fighter jet is a demanding schedule. In addition, crew chiefs have to be able to function in any environment where planes take off and land. McFadden, who works at Misawa Air Base in Japan, describes his job on the *Air Force Live* blog: "You can say 'It's cold, it's hard, it's dirty, I bust my knuckles, I'm always in the elements,' but you can't truly understand it until you're out here."

Earnings

Crew chiefs are paid according to the Air Force's standardized pay scale, which is based on pay grade and years in service. They also receive free or discount housing and medical and dental care.

Opportunities for Advancement

After completing the initial technical school coursework, airmen earn the lowest rank of airman basic (E-1) and progress to senior airman (E-4). After completing on-the-job training, gaining experience, and earning weighted airman points, crew chiefs will typically advance through the ranks to master sergeant (E-7). These individuals can earn additional professional certifications—becoming certified production technicians, Federal Aviation Administration–certified airframe or power plant mechanics, or certified aerospace technicians—for career advancement and promotion opportunities.

What Is the Future Outlook for a Crew Chief?

A single combat aircraft can cost a whopping $200 million. When it breaks down in a remote battlefield, the crew chief is the first person called. The Air Force realizes the value of these individuals; it was expected to request a 2016 budget that included hiring four thousand more airmen. Many of these positions were expected to be in the aircraft maintenance field. According to a September 2015 *Air Force Magazine Daily Report* blog, the Air Force was trying to fill the many maintenance field vacancies just to meet the minimum standards of safety determined by the Department of Defense. Therefore, aircraft maintenance crews are in demand, and crew chiefs are needed to direct these crews.

What Are Employment Prospects in the Civilian World?

Commercial airlines are always on the lookout for qualified former airmen to fill maintenance vacancies. The *Air Force Times* reported in April 2015 that Southwest Airlines is one of the most active recruiters. "Maintainers from the Air Force and other service branches, airlines say, come with years of experience working on complicated air frames," the report attests. "They're usually disciplined, reliable, accustomed to working in tough situations and handling stress, and can both lead and work well as a team." Smaller companies also hire crew chiefs to provide mechanical and electrical service repair and custom designs for private, commercial, and military aircraft.

Hiring a crew chief with an Air Force background is very useful to commercial employers because these prospects are already adept at diagnosing and resolving technical problems, managing subordinate staff, and understanding the systems utilized on multiple types of aircraft. Thus, crew chiefs can make the transition from military craft to commercial craft fairly easily. Their ability to spot potential problems, carry out routine inspections, and control a team of mechanics make them excellent hires.

Logistics Planner

What Does a Logistics Planner Do?

Everything that happens in the Air Force requires planning and coordination. Logistics planners work behind the scenes to make sure missions run smoothly and that service members stay safe. They encompass a large group of specialists. Some deal exclusively with the processing of paperwork. Others handle agreements between the Air Force and its suppliers. Some are responsible for managing all the cargo, equipment, and supplies the Air Force needs to stay combat ready. Equipment and supplies can be anything from small parts needed to repair a computer to ammunition for aircraft and even cargo trucks needed to transport items. They have to make sure the Air Force always has enough of any supply item in case of emergencies. Because this is such a big job, it is broken down into smaller responsibilities. For example, one group of planners is in charge of the trucks, cars, and other transports needed to move cargo and personnel. They have to ensure that all these vehicles are accounted for and operational at all times. This includes keeping track of fuel supplies and parts.

Gasoline and diesel are not the only kinds of fuel they are

At a Glance:
Logistics Planner

Minimum Educational Requirements
High school diploma or GED

Personal Qualities
Organized, good planner, analytical, resourceful

Working Conditions
Flight lines, science labs, office settings

Salary Range
Monthly salary depends on pay grade and years of service

Future Outlook
22 percent job growth through 2022

responsible for. At Air Force cryogenics labs, logistics planners manage liquid nitrogen and liquid oxygen reserves. Liquid nitrogen is used to temporarily shrink mechanical parts that need to be put together for a tight seal in aircraft. Liquid oxygen is used by pilots during flight missions at 10,000 feet (3,048 m) and higher because, unlike commercial airliners, their aircraft are not pressurized. These types of fuels must be kept at -50°F (-46°C), which means that logistics teams work in very cold conditions when they are checking on supplies. Dustin Volpi, a logistics planner and fuels distribution supervisor, handles and manages liquid nitrogen and oxygen in order to maintain operational readiness for his base's aircraft. He explains how much he loves his job on the Department of Defense's *Armed with Science* blog. "It's a fun job. You get to work with stuff that nobody else in the Air Force does," Volpi says. "Even though there is no real way to compensate for the cold, it's part of your job—so you just deal with it and press at it."

The important job of keeping track of weapons and ammunition is assigned to another group of detail-oriented professionals, who develop and manage entire weapons systems and the equipment needed to keep them operational. Major Zev York, a logistics readiness squadron commander at Barksdale Air Force Base in Louisiana, leads logistics planners in organizing the deployment of almost three hundred troops and their cargo overseas each year. His squadron also oversees the weapons vault. It is accountable for issuing and tracking all weapons assigned to airmen during deployment to make sure no weapon or munition falls into the wrong hands.

While keeping each stateside Air Force base organized takes a lot of planning, organizing, and coordinating, logistics planners have to also keep track of airmen, equipment, cargo, and supplies that are deployed throughout the world. They make sure that all personnel preparing to deploy have completed required training and that personal information on file with the Air Force is up to date. They may not be on the frontline in combat; however, they diligently and precisely plan and coordinate the movements of people, supplies, and equipment for all missions. Starting months in advance of the actual deployment date, a logistics team is put into place to figure out the best way for aircraft, troops, equipment, and supplies to arrive when and where they are needed. Logistics planners at Nevada's Nellis Air Force Base are kept very busy preparing airmen who are being deployed. Each year they organize between fifteen hundred to two thousand airmen for deployment. They make sure that everything is in order before airmen leave for a tour of duty. This includes confirming that their personal paperwork is accurate and up to date and that any hands-on training required for the mission is complete. In addition, logistics planners are responsible for coordinating the food and lodging orders for airmen who are being deployed. They also ensure that all supplies arrive at the deployment mission location. "There is a lot that has to happen in the pre-deployment stages before an Airman can leave," explains logistics planner Kelvin Valle in a 2015 *Air Force Print News Today* article. He knows how vital his team's role is to the overall success of the mission.

How Do You Become a Logistics Planner?

Education

Entry into this specialty requires a high school diploma or its equivalent; however, coursework or a college degree in logistics and transportation or business is highly desirable. To prepare for this career choice, joining the Air Force Junior Reserve Officers' Training Corps (AFJROTC) is a step in the right direction. Every AFJROTC squadron has a logistics officer. Along with five other officer positions, they report directly to the deputy corps commander. Their duties include issuing and accounting; maintaining, repairing, and cleaning all equipment; and maintaining receipts and keeping records for all AFJROTC uniforms, equipment, and supplies. In addition to gaining experience in logistics, anyone interested in this field who is a member of the AFJROTC will attend the Air Force–approved course on leadership, team building, and character education—all skills required for a logistics readiness squadron career path.

For enlisted personnel, logistics planning begins at the apprentice level with the Introduction to Logistics Course. During this class, students are introduced to the basics of Air Force logistics, which includes processing, organizing, and issuing equipment and supplies. They practice the important behind-the-scenes procedures that make the Air Force run smoothly. Students also learn how to use the Logistics Module, the online database used for keeping track of all Air Force equipment and supplies. The final step in becoming a logistics planner is to complete on-the-job training at a logistics readiness squadron like the one at Luke Air Force Base in Arizona. Logistics planners who make it through may then be assigned to co-ordinate and track Air Force cargo such as aircraft parts, deployment matériel, and even explosives and ammunition. Making sure these supplies reach their destination in a timely and safe manner is the overall goal of these logistics planners.

Volunteer Work and Internship

To get started in this career while still in school, students can participate in organizing events such as fund-raisers, school carnivals, or plays. Anything that requires coordinating people and supplies can give a taste of what's in store for a career in military logistics. Working behind the scenes to make sure events come off without trouble—or even addressing problems as they arise—are exactly the qualities that can prepare an individual for what lies ahead as a logistics planner.

Skills and Personality

The Air Force depends on logistics planners for getting the right people, equipment, and supplies to the right place at the right time. It is the job of logistics planners to make sure that all of those elements are in place so that the mission can be carried out smoothly and safely. The men and women who do this work must be extremely well organized, methodical, and detail oriented. They must be able to anticipate problems and find solutions. They must have strong math and computer skills and be able to deal with deadlines and stressful situations. Because not every mission goes off without a hitch, logistics planners should also be calm and resourceful enough to respond to problems as they arise. Often the most successful planners are not those who aim for perfection but those who can respond to any contingency and still get the job done.

On the Job

Working Conditions

Most logistics planners work in an office setting at bases all over the country. They are assigned to logistics readiness squadrons that handle a variety of tasks. Although they work traditional office hours from nine to five, they are also expected to be ready to work at any time. If a vehicle needs an emergency repair during a combat mission, logistics planners will be called to duty to find and coordinate the delivery of the right parts. Therefore, many days can be stressful in the workplace, carrying out an assigned task on a tight deadline.

Earnings

Monthly salary depends on pay grade and years in service. Logistics planners are also provided free or discount housing and medical and dental care.

Opportunities for Advancement

After completing their initial coursework in logistics, airmen earn the lowest enlisted rank of apprentice, airman basic. Apprentice-level planners usually begin their career as the point of contact for managing and processing paperwork or coordinating services and matériel for the Air Force with civilian companies. They will make sure the Air Force is getting a fair deal. Once they have completed their apprenticeship, they can be promoted to airman first class, or journeyman. At this stage, logistics planning skills are advanced through completion of online career development courses. Journeymen are responsible for organizing housing and arranging vehicle assignments and deployments. Before being promoted to the next level, craftsman, they must also complete the War Reserve Matériel Program course and attend Airman Leadership School. As a craftsman, logistics planners will continue taking advanced coursework on contingency wartime planning and combat logistics along with completing additional career development courses online. Promotion to superintendent requires advanced coursework in budget, manpower, and resource and personnel management. These positions oversee larger projects, each with an extensive staff to help accomplish the assigned duty.

What Is the Future Outlook for a Logistics Planner?

The *Air Force Times* reports that budget increases will allow for an additional 4,020 active-duty positions through 2017 in an effort to strengthen intelligence, surveillance, and reconnaissance capabilities. These missions will require logistics planners to organize all aspects of training and combat missions, including transportation, cargo, and personnel. Therefore, prospects in logistics will grow as these capabilities expand.

What Are Employment Prospects in the Civilian World?

The Council of Logistics Management states that logistics was the second-largest employment sector in the United States as of 2013, with executive management earning well over six figures. Employment opportunities exist in merchandising firms, consulting firms, government agencies, transportation firms, third-party logistics firms, and manufacturing firms. To these employers, former Air Force logistic planners can offer valuable experience along with the added benefits of self-discipline, leadership, and teamwork that come from military training.

Retired major general Lew Curtis successfully transitioned from military to civilian life as a private logistics consultant with Daytona Aerospace, a company that provides logistics strategizing, planning, and analysis to create public and private aircraft partnerships. Retired logistics readiness officer Monique Johnson found herself facing new challenges as a sourcing program leader for GE Aviation, where she manages the production, processing, and sales of General Electric products. During an interview with Orion International, a military talent placement firm, Johnson stated that her military training taught her to adapt to any environment and to any group of people. "It also equipped me with the can-do attitude and to draw from past experiences to elevate me to the next level of success," Johnson said. Having that type of confidence—coupled with a military career that demands excellence—makes logistics planners a top choice for civilian employers.

Interview with a Crew Chief

Troy Altevers is a recently retired crew chief production superintendent with the Air Force. He served twenty years active duty before retiring in May 2015. Altevers has deployed to every major combat zone since 1996, including Iraq and Afghanistan. He spoke with the author by phone about his military career and recent transition to the civilian workforce.

Q: Why did you join the Air Force?

A: My parents were poor and I wanted to go to college. I also wanted to serve my country. With the GI Bill, I knew that the military would pay for my college degree. My dad was Air Force, his brothers were Army, his sister was Navy, and many of my cousins on my father's side of the family have served in the military.

Q: Why did you become a crew chief?

A: I joined the Air Force when I was eighteen years old but signed up for delayed enlistment when I was seventeen. I was given five options for a career path, including weapons, security forces, and crew chief. About three-quarters of the way through basic training we were all given our assignments. I got crew chief on the F-15—the best airplane in the world. It has never been defeated in air-to-air combat in its history. This was my first choice of careers because I love airplanes and working with my hands. I did what only 2 percent of the population will ever see or do; it's just amazing.

Q: How did you train for this career?

A: After basic training, the initial crew chief training was about four months where I learned everything about flight line maintenance and then got assigned to an aircraft. Mine was an F-15 fighter; I put my name on it and it was my responsibility to fix and maintain. A lot has changed since then; now most of the training is OJT [on-the-job training].

In the beginning I was a glorified mechanic on one aircraft. If it didn't need work or maintenance then I helped another crew chief on a different jet. I started out as an airman basic and worked my way through the ranks to master sergeant, which took fifteen years of service. I was in charge of all the career fields responsible for the production side of the flight line and making sure that all the jets were on schedule.

Q: Can you describe your typical workday?

A: Since 1996, I have been deployed all over the world to every major conflict, where I worked on airplanes during combat operations. When I worked on a base in the US, I was in charge of preparing all the aircraft in my flight line for training missions.

Q: What do you like most and least about your job?

A: I really like the uniqueness of the production side of my job, especially when one of my airplanes comes back from a combat mission and I can see the results of my hard work. Later in my career my flight line included the U-2S, a reconnaissance aircraft that carries a lot of unique and different systems that can listen to bad guys and does a lot of cool spy stuff. Every person has an EPR—enlisted performance report, where they were rated on a scale from one to five. The supervisor reviewed their team and then I had to proofread and correct everyone on the flight line. I hated that part.

Q: What personal qualities do you find most valuable for this type of work?

A: You have to be disciplined and adapt quickly because in my career things change so quickly. Everything might be working smooth and then all of a sudden there is an in-flight emergency or a jet ready to fly and something needs to be fixed. If you can't get it fixed then another aircraft needs to be prepared right away. This is a very stressful job, but for me, I am happiest when working under pressure. It kept me challenged and gave me a sense of accomplishment.

Q: What advice do you have for high school students who might be interested in this career?
A: If you want to see the world and something you'll never see as a civilian, this is the best job. I've seen some of the coolest things ever; the airplanes themselves are awesome. Without us, there is no Air Force.

Find Out More

About Careers: US Military
website: http://usmilitary.about.com/od/airforcejoin

Written in user-friendly terms, this website provides information about how to enlist in the Air Force and discusses the educational requirements and working conditions for a variety of enlisted and officer careers.

Bureau of Labor Statistics (BLS)
website: www.bls.gov/ooh/military/military-careers.htm

The BLS is the official government website that is responsible for gathering and posting information related to working conditions and job outlook. The military section provides information on current enlisted and officer careers in the Air Force.

Military.com
website: www.military.com

Military.com provides up-to-date information about military news and technology, job vacancies, and the benefits of service.

O*NET OnLine
website: www.onetonline.org/crosswalk/MOC

By choosing a branch of the military along with a job title, this webpage provides a comprehensive list of the professional and personal skills it takes for the career along with job openings and related occupations.

Today's Military
website: http://todaysmilitary.com/joining/air-force

The Department of Defense developed this resource for parents, teachers, and students interested in a career in the military. Information includes benefits, careers, and salaries for joining the Air Force.

US Air Force
website: www.airforce.com

This is the official website of the Air Force. The careers section provides information on a variety of careers organized by areas of interest.

Other Jobs in the Air Force

Aerospace maintenance
Air battle manager
Air transportation
Airborne Mission Systems
   Operation
Aircrew Flight equipment
Airfield Management
Avionics systems
Band officer
Bioenvironmental engineering
Broadcast journalist
Cable and antenna support
Chaplain officer
Civil engineer
Clinical social worker
Combat control
Computer systems
   programming
Critical care physician

Critical care nurse
Cryptologic language analyst
Cybertransport systems
Dental assistant
Diagnostic radiologist
Dietitian
Emergency medicine physician
Explosive ordnance disposal
Fire protection
Occupational medicine specialist
Pediatrician
Psychiatrist
Public health officer
Safety specialist
Space and missile operations
   officer
Space systems operations
Special missions aviation

Index

About the Author

Melissa Phillips is a professor of special education and positive behavior interventions. She lives in San Diego with her son, husband, and two dogs. In her spare time she likes spending time outdoors with her family.